Wandering Through The Fire

A Journey of Pain and Purpose
Volume 1 - The Awakening

Cyrus Cormier

ISBN: 978-1-945990-64-9

Published by High Tide Publications, Inc.
www.hightidepublications.com

Thank you for purchasing an authorized edition of Wandering Through the Fire.

High Tide's mission is to find, encourage, promote, and publish the work of authors. We are a small, woman-owned enterprise that is dedicated to the author over 50. When you buy an authorized copy, you help us to bring their work to you.

We thank you for supporting our authors.

Edited by Cindy L. Freeman
Book Design by Firebellied Frog Graphic Design www.firebelliedfrog.com

To the people who raised me, taught me, encouraged me, pushed me, comforted me, and loved me unconditionally

Foreword

Being ourselves in the world is what we want in life, but such is seldom easy or even not possible for some. We move into and out of things, sometimes bruised and needing a pep talk. It's a struggle to survive, but we all have self-knowledge so we must be honest with ourselves as we move.. We see paths emerging ahead of us as we look for opportunity and reward. To be your true self is the greatest wish that I could make for humankind - to be your authentic self, honest to thyself.

The life and times of Cyrus began for me the day we met at his family's fish market in Houston back in the early seventies, back when we were raw, young with only callous on our hands. His personality smiled across the counter while he was butchering fish as I was being greeted by his mama – we met on the job, if you will.

Our life paths paralleled one another's in that hiring authorities recognized our potential or character above our degrees or credentials, thus opening doors for us into which to shine. You must earn it, and he did.

His potential was apparent to others, his performance was hard-earned while he remained helpful to his fellow associates. Always in his life, he has lent a helping hand to others, some of whom he met on his first job and whom he mentors still.

Finally, I know the introverted person who is Cyrus, a person blessed with emotional intelligence and of good character; coming through generations of his loving and hard-working family who made their way outward from Bayou Teche into Houston and provided their children with education and standing. Indeed, the central theme of this book is love as he reveals to you in the sincerity of his words, in the pain and joy that he has lived, and in the forgiveness that is authentic self. This is my friend Cyrus.

Bill Cunningham
Wichita Mountains
Southwest Oklahoma

Table of Contents

Chapter 1

Scars in My Soul

The Will to Do and the Courage to Be

I grew up Black in the inner city of Houston with heritage from Southern Louisiana. It was a time of racial integration that carved a gumbo of cultures into the fabric of who I was to become. With my humble beginnings, many wants went unfulfilled, but all needs were infused with loving kindness as I considered my life's situation better than most. My values consisted of God, family, education, work, food, food, and food. Well, I *am* of Creole descent.

Life never came easy nor was I ever privileged or abundantly talented. Rather, I was sufficiently gifted to elevate above average in most things. My fortune in life took the form of a mother, father, and grandfather who modeled resilience and determination. Each of them helped to pave my path toward taking a little and making plenty of my inner self. My mother poured education, compassion, and kindness into my being. My father filled my boots with the courage to step into my dreams, and my grandfather showed me how sheer will was the ammunition needed to overcome any limitations.

It was these modest beginnings and the people who molded me that birthed my mantra, "The will to do and the courage to be." If I *will* it, I can *do* it. Regardless of my skill level, I can overachieve in this life if I try harder and become more resilient and more determined than most. It also means I must be fearless in life, but I must be kind, compassionate, and faithful. Most of all, I must be authentically me. The will to *do* makes the impossible possible, and the courage to *be* makes me unapologetically who I am meant to be.

Fear and Faith

My first recollection of fear is also my first memory of many racist incidents in my life. One summer day while spending time with my grandfather in the racially charged 1963 Louisiana town of St. Martinsville, my grandfather and I went to town where we were confronted by a group of men that threw taunts of racial slurs toward us. I was only five or six years old, and while I could not comprehend the situation in its entirety, I could understand that the color of skin was the line of division of civility, equality, violence, and oppression. While I stood there firmly gripping my grandfather's hand, fear raged through my being, and all I could hear were the Creole words with which he responded to their taunts. "*Bondye Savyar*," he said. Translated into English, this means, "God Savior." Smiling at the men, he repeated those words, never looking away until they eventually left us without further incident.

To give background to the situation, my grandfather was a victim of an accident years before. Falling into a sugar cane mill, he lost an arm and cut one leg severely, causing him to walk with a limp. He was only four-foot-eleven and weighed maybe 130 pounds. He was physically limited but faithfully limitless.

As I recall this encounter, I realize it traumatized me. Although I never articulated it to him or anyone else until recently, I have lived with the pain of it my entire life. The encounter was emotionally transformative for me. It left me with fear of what people might do to other people just because of their skin color. I also felt confused about what and who I was. I experienced shame that my grandfather didn't stand up to the racist men. Then my shame turned to anger that anyone would do this to my family and me. Guilt followed anger. Guilt that I could be ashamed of my grandfather for not standing up to those men, especially with his physical limitations.

Eventually, I was able to achieve forgiveness, forgiving myself for my negative feelings and lack of awareness and understanding as a child.

From forgiveness, I moved to conviction, the conviction to tell another child, another man, another racist, that the color line of division will not define me; it will only refine me--refine me to live with self-awareness, self-confidence, and self-love. Today, I understand that my grandfather didn't fear those men and didn't fear death. Rather, he feared what might happen to me, and this was his way of protecting me. Almost sixty years later the line of division called skin color still exists. Now, like my grandfather, I cry "Bondye Savyar," and I add, "Black Lives Matter."

This brings to mind the end of one of Robert Frost's poems:

> "The rain to the wind said,
> 'You push and I'll pelt.'
> They so smote the garden bed.
> That the flowers actually knelt,
> And lay lodged—though not dead.
> I know how the flowers felt."

How Far Can We Go?

What is "will" and how far can it take us? It depends on how far we are willing to go. I watched my grandfather exceed the expectations the world placed on him. He was the size of a twelve-year-old. He was a one-armed, black man living in a racially charged town in South Louisiana from the late 1800s to late 1900s. His nearly one hundred years of life bear proof that "will" is one of the key ingredients to succeeding in life. To provide for his family, he played the clarinet in a band, drove his car as a taxi, farmed his land, and raised livestock. With so many things working against him, he defeated the odds through sheer will, overcoming all obstacles that came his way. What were the lessons I learned from this warrior?

At times, we may be weary, we may be lazy, we may be selfish, we may be self-centered, but when we move past those things and stay centered and determined we find the will to do. We know we can do much more, but all too often we become prisoners to life's pressures. We get too comfortable doing the things that don't matter, too comfortable doing nothing, too comfortable holding back instead of moving forward, thus losing focus of what we should be doing. We place ourselves in tiny boxes where big dreams can't breathe, but we have the capacity to go beyond the box of smallness. This world has taught us to think in terms of the now, the today, the here and there, but there is more to see when we open our eyes and think beyond the self-imposed ceilings we lock ourselves into. Adopting the will to do is having the will to make possible the impossible. The will to do is being fearless, committed, and persistent to push through the closed doors in our minds. The will to do is about having faith in who we are and who we can become. The will to do is seeing the unseen, hearing what no one else can hear, and speaking what has never been spoken. The will to do is going farther and fighting through the pain, fighting through the doubt, fighting through limits and arriving at the limitless avenue.

My grandfather fought through racism, handicap, lack of education, and injustice. He pushed through the ceilings the world tried to place on him. How far can you go? As far as you are willing to go. My grandfather taught me to be mindful, determined, and resilient--to let my will drive me to be me.

Authenticity

There are eight billion people in the world, and each of us has a different fingerprint. This is evidence that we are all unique. Our uniqueness calls us to find something, do something, and be something that only we cast out into the universe. Find that, do that, and be that. Place your fingerprint on the world. The most courageous thing you can ever do in life is to be you, authentically you.

I spent most of my young adult life wearing masks to fit in, to be liked, to be considered normal for whatever definition normal bears. The world places unrealistic expectations on all of us, and I was no different. Growing up black in an inner city black neighborhood during the 60s and 70s placed on me expectations of being an athlete with plenty of girlfriends, hanging out with the fellows, listening to soul music, and attending parties. These were the main staples for the dinner of my portrayal. My passion for writing, learning, public speaking, and activism were muted over the loud cry for acceptance by the tribe of my environment.

Hiding behind the mask of inclusion suppressed the real me. I paid with pain and anguish, and the sting pushed me deeper and deeper into inner reflection as I began to block the world. An outer smile and occasional meaningless conversations were but the temporary distractions of a child hurting from not allowing his true light to shine.

The constant running away from self drove me to a distant dark destination with scattered thoughts and reckless emotions. There I found no one to talk to but the man in the mirror. Because this man was broken, he provided no comfort. Rather, he suggested hints of destructive escapism. I surrounded myself with busyness. But busyness brought me only more discomfort and problems as I fell further and further away from my authenticity.

My life was tumbling toward introversion's doorstep, leading me ever-so-close to a room of reclusion. It was taboo for Blacks to even think about seeking mental help or therapy. It was equally taboo for a black man to cry and surrender to emotions. After all, black men were meant to be tried and tested; and unjust justice was a daily occurrence. The appearance of weakness had no seat at the black man's table.

I continued to smile until I could smile no more, hide until I ran out of hiding places, laugh until laughter's bucket was emptied. My uncried tears finally gave way after many years of adopting a fake persona. Finally, when I could no longer carry the burden of false identity, my authentic self could no longer be suppressed. I hungered to find the courage to be--to be me. The call to courage was so compelling it could neither be ignored nor extinguished. Gradually, it gave way to the emergence of Cyrus...the real Cyrus. I realized it was okay to be who I was meant to be regardless of how my world viewed and judged me. I learned to never try to fit in; my nature was created to fit naturally and so was yours.

Find your nature and wear it well. It fits only you.

Fighting Through the Pain

Scarred physically is my promise of death, scarred emotionally is my proof of living. Tirelessly I press forward with unwavering determination, scarred but not scared.

Cyrus

We all are inexplicably caught in the never-ending battles of emotional and physical pain throughout our lives. To say I've had my fair share of fights would be an understatement of epic proportions. One such emotional battle occurred when I was in the fourth grade. My mother, ever the educator, wanted the best for her children including education. With our meager finances, the best education meant sending us to a private Catholic school.

The year was 1967 and the Catholic school was in downtown Houston. This was my introduction to private school as well as racial integration. Of the less than ten Blacks attending this school, two were my siblings and one was myself. I guess you could consider this situation more of a sprinkle of diversity than true integration. As a child, I already struggled with introversion, and going to a new school placed my consciousness far out of my comfort zone. At times it seemed too great a burden to bear.

Classroom sizes were small--less than fifteen--and although there was another Black person in the room, I was the focal point of the stares from my white classmates. The other Black person was a girl whose skin was as ivory as any white person's, and her hair texture indicated European descent. For me, there was an ever-present pressure of answering questions, speaking, competing, and taking tests. Exceeding average was not an option, but rather a requirement with a mother like mine and siblings with better-than-average intellect. Having a total of zero friends in class or in the school made it more difficult to assimilate into student activities and build any normal childhood relationships.

One day our class was taking a test. I was prepared and confident as I finished my test before most. Having to use the restroom, I asked the teacher if I could be excused, but I was denied. She stated that after everyone finished the test, I would be allowed to go. I took my seat, and after what felt like an eternity, I got up again and pleaded with my teacher to be excused...only to be denied again. As I sat in my seat, the urge became uncontrollable, and I peed on myself. As urine puddled on the floor beneath me and the other kids stared at me, my teacher caught a glimpse of what had happened. She excused the class, leaving me embarrassed and alone in a world of shame. The teacher called my mother who drove to the school with a change of clothes and a bag of not-so-nice words for the teacher.

Returning to school the next day and the rest of that year was one of the hardest things I had to endure. Already an outcast, now felt like I was diseased with leprosy or some other deadly affliction. I sat alone in the classroom, alone on the playground, and alone in the lunchroom. Every day I felt like the pain was greater than the day before and the day before that. I was forced to shoulder shame with no end in sight. As fortune would have it, due to the school's financial turmoil, the institution closed at the end of that year.

The following year I returned to public school, the same school I had come from in the same neighborhood, but nothing was ever the same with me. This experience changed my life forever. If I suffered from introversion before, now it was more on a level of being a recluse. I often wondered why my teacher didn't let me go to the restroom. Was it because I was Black? Why didn't I just get up and leave and accept her consequences rather than enduring the humiliation? There are too many questions and not enough answers. But living in a tormented past permits me no growth. I was and never will be the same person I was before this event, and the thing is, I don't want to be. The lessons I learned were too valuable for me to miss, lessons about overcoming shame, acquiring confidence and becoming resilient. I take all these lessons as armor for my life's journey as I do battle with pride and ego both internally and externally.

Truly, I'm scarred but no longer scared.

Chapter 2

Fire Raging

Stay Present

Imprisoned by the chains of economics, the window of exposure to the world was a closed curtain. It was limited to where I lived in Houston and my parents' hometowns in Louisiana. During my childhood, our family had only one vacation, but an adventure followed our every move. We would leave Houston and travel to Southern California to visit relatives, with various stops along the way. Excitement filled the then eight-year-old boy going somewhere I had never been, seeing things I had never seen, and visiting cousins I had never met. Our car was loaded with the few pieces of luggage we owned and seven occupants. Our family was off for what I thought would be the adventure of a lifetime.

Seven people in a Chevy sedan traveling unfamiliar highways, passing through new cities and towns was almost more than my young heart could stand. Hotels and motels were not an option on our limited budget, so Mom and Dad alternated driving, and it felt like our car never stopped. Our first stop was Lincoln, Nebraska to visit one of my father's sisters. I remember very little about Nebraska or staying with my aunt. I can't even remember her name. I do remember the fresh air, the cornfields, the small towns and one memorable stop for gas.

Stopping at a small town's general store to get gas, we were visited by the customers who came outside to look at us. They had never seen any Black people, and their curious stares were intimidating. My limited understanding of the situation brought with it both fear and shame.

People gazing at us as if we were alien forms or animals in a zoo seemed condescending, like they viewed us as inferior. Continuing down the road, our car was consumed with silence and sadness as our parents tried to change the subject and guide our consciousness to a more palatable discussion. But we pressed forward to my aunt's house, never to forget the dividing line of color that was ever present.

Our second stop of consequence was the famous Four Corners where Utah, Colorado, Arizona, and New Mexico all met. We ran around and played, fascinated by the fact that we could leave and enter four states in a matter of seconds. The mystery of the Southwest where we had never ventured was enhanced by the abundant beauty of mountains and desert, neither of which we had ever seen. Recognition of a world bigger than what I had known would peak an insatiable appetite for travel. Onward we went to our next destination: Las Vegas. The only thing I knew about the city was that it was a place to gamble, and gambling was a topic of discontentment between my mother and father.

As far as the eye could see, Vegas appeared as endless miles of hotels and casinos. I sat in the car listening to my parents' vigorous conversation about money and gambling. Finally, my mother yielded to my father's wishes and gave him a couple of traveler's checks. Filled with delusion and the optimism of winning the big one, Dad entered and exited the casino within a matter of minutes, minus the currency and the win. Our next stop was sunny California where I thought only the rich lived, movie stars and millionaires, and I was not sure how I could possibly have any cousins living there.

We arrived in California late at night and waking up in the car, all I could see was fire everywhere. Cars on fire, buildings on fire, even fire stations on fire. People running, police all over the place, sirens blaring, and smoke filling the air--not the California I had pictured. Slowly and carefully driving through the mayhem, we finally arrived at my aunt's home where we asked what was going on. My aunt lived in a city called Watts and we had driven through the Watts Riot of 1965. This riot was precipitated by the violent arrest of a black man where police not only beat him but also his mother who was trying to stop them from hurting her son. Police brutality of black men was an all-too-common occurrence then, and fifty-six years later, we find ourselves in the same situation.

There are varying views on police brutality, police reform, and the new term of "defund" the police. No matter the view, the scene should and must change. My one and only vacation as a child was an adventure never to be forgotten with sights of beauty and sights of horror. The trip gave me as much as it took away from me, and I hold it deep in my heart, what once was and what is today. The uncommon times that lacked humanity are mirrored by the common times of today's injustices. I have had many vacations as an adult, but none have been more indelible in my memory than this one.

The past gallops into the present and takes stake, robbing us of our now. We must find strength in the pain of yesterday, search for a better tomorrow, and be courageous in the present.

The Color of Skin

The color of skin remains a major line of division in civility, equality, violence, oppression, inclusivity, and decency. This separation is not just between Black and White but also between Black and Black. The neighborhood of my youth was all Black, and most people's roots were either in Texas or Louisiana. The struggle for classification and equality was at times just as powerful within race as it was between races.

The deep South brought with it a defilement of skin color, vernacular, hair texture, and facial features. People from Southern Louisiana had an accent from their native Creole that sounded like a combination of French and English that people from Texas would mock. This language disparity was taken as a sign of inferiority and could be cause for banishment within a racial divide. Instead of embracing one's own language and culture, people would try to disguise who they were for the sake of inclusion and equal opportunity. Instead of celebrating their culture and passing it onto the next generation, many Blacks suppressed their heritage. Whites looked down on Blacks as inferior and some Blacks looked down on other Blacks as inferior, creating an imaginary bottom of the bottom.

My Louisiana heritage carried the weight of classification, placing me in the bucket of less-than. Considered inferior by all races, even my own, I was compelled to fight for respect, trying to dispel the notion of inferiority. I know now that I was not less-than. I was great in my own skin for who I was. I was taller than most, faster than most, intellectually more capable than many. I was creative, determined, and capable. Yet I was lonely, with a constant feeling of helplessness. The fellas in my neighborhood were merciless. It was not a place for the weak or meek. The taunting, teasing, joking, bullying, and sports competitiveness, could at times be too much, yet this was my world, and bowing out was never an option.

Here I was with my reddish-brown skin, Louisiana heritage, with Creole-speaking, overprotective parents who pushed me to excel in school. I was an athlete with few real friends, and an introvert to boot. I was all of this and I was nothing because none of these characteristics defined me or recognized my hidden passion to write. After all, a Black male writer living in the hood would certainly draw more abuse from the homies. So, I wrote in secret and immediately threw away my literary creations. I was a dreamer, a thinker, a philosopher, who believed that one day the world would change, that people would love and respect each other, and the color of skin would not define, separate, or discriminate.

The color of skin is real, it is still a determining factor in friends, marriages, jobs, and equality, to name a few. Race is more than just color, it's also height, weight, and any of the other outward features we are born with. For a child overcoming the insanity of pain inflicted by others--because you are who you are, the person you were born to be, who you have the right to be--can be catastrophic. I was not the only one who had to endure oppression, but in my mind, I was carrying the weight of the world on my shoulders. The thing about carrying weight is, if you survive and don't give up, it makes you stronger. I got stronger but not until much later in life. I am who I am because I was made by the Great I AM, and it's with this confidence and courage that I walk strong, I love strong, and I am strong.

The only person you must be better than is the person you were yesterday.

Damaged but not Done

The superficial detection of identity is but a microcosm of the discovery of self, in the treasure hunt that we call life. Identity combines gender, name, sexual orientation, race, and nationality. More importantly, identity is how we project to the world and how the world views us. Discovery of self is a lifelong pursuit, ever changing, reflective, relative, subjective, complicated, and often misinterpreted.

My life was quickly spiraling out of control as I questioned my very existence, purpose, and destiny. These thoughts were all too contemplative for a young mind as I began the exhausting search for self. The journey was paradoxically both stimulating and numbing as I held an optimistic view of capturing this elusive self in some short time.

The curiosity of the *why* fascinated my imagination as I assumed if I could only answer the *why* in everything, including self, the answers of the universe would lay bare. Why am I here? Why was I born this way? Why do people hate each other? Why is there so much pain in the world? The more I lived, the more it felt like I was being damaged by the messy things of life and by other people. Damage to my ego, damage to my persona, damage to my path of self-discovery, damage to opportunity, damage to everything I either wanted or needed. It seemed so unfair but inevitable with the next wrecking ball at each sunrise. No one had prepared me for this roller-coaster. I felt I was put on the ride with no seatbelt. With every twist and turn the ride threw at me, the hill of damage turned into a mountain until damage knocked at my soul's door.

At first, daunted by damage's razor-sharp edge, finally I pressed forward in search of self, thinking that would be the key to freedom. Clutched in the grasp of what I thought the world expected of me, I allowed damage to continue its ruthless infliction. The irony of searching for self on the one hand, yet not having the courage to go outside the boundaries of normality to be my true self is what caused damage to take hold. To the mirror of my reflection, I begged the question:

Mirror mirror on the wall.

Why is life so hard; why do I continue to fall?

The search for self is a never-ending quest,

I need to know who I am to be my very best.

Mirror mirror on the wall to whom I once starred,

Uncried tears fill my eyes, and I can barely glare.

Life taunts and hurts me just for fun,

I'm beat and damaged but I am not done.

Too many days of looking in the mirror with unanswered questions left me withered, but my steps must carry on. I am damaged, but not done.

Self-Forgiveness

As the saying goes, "If I knew then what I know now..." forgiveness of self would have precluded many heartaches. Now, I can glance back and stare forward with me forgiving me unapologetically. The following is a fast-forward into a better future. Rather than holding it for later, I am compelled to share it now in hopes that someone can use it, hold on to it, believe it, and become better for it. Today I say, "I forgive me."

I forgive myself, and I loosen the bondage of normality and conformity that has reduced my being to a shell half empty and not yet half full. I must break the chain of questions that have imprisoned my thoughts and kept me in a cell of hollowness. The pretentious smiles I offer daily beg me to ponder if those reciprocating are also suffering. Surely I'm not the only one feeling lost in the false existence of enslavement to the expectations of a world diseased with greed, a world that seems to dictate its artificial expectation of success. What are we doing; why are we lying to ourselves; how can we release ourselves to the freedom of a happier whole person, empty of judgment or self-induced conviction? The absolution that I seek must come from within, but the journey to the place where this forgiveness resides often appears too difficult a road to travel. The many years of denial and suppression have taught me to flee to a safer space and time, a place devoid of deep self-reflection wherein lies acknowledgment of guilt and imperfection. My attempted escape from this tortuous place leads me nowhere as I dwell in a vicious cycle of nothingness.

Repenting through deeds of goodwill or words of humility and teaching others how to sidestep life's pitfalls provides only momentary relief. The lasting peace I seek dwells in an unfulfilled destination. Someone urges my footsteps toward not the forgiveness of a bitter world, but forgiveness of me. The clock continues to tick, and, as I glance in the mirror, it becomes a race against time to find my authentic self and pardon myself for my brokenness.

I have wrongly assumed that life's mirror is cracked when the actualization of my own brokenness haunts me with ghosts of shame and ego. Tick tock goes the clock as the pace of the race increases with every fleeting moment. I submerge deeper and deeper into despair as I pass life's baton from who me, to why me, to fake me, and finally, to authentic me. Only then am I ready for the final lap that leads to forgiven me. Along the way, I fumble the baton with every clumsy step until, in the distance, I see the tape of peace that beckons me toward the finish line.

Forgiveness is not that masked villain too often equated with admission of guilt. Rather forgiveness of self is the saving hero that brings me to wholeness. My race is not over nor is my quest for grasping the baton of life, but with the act of self-forgiveness, the winds of epiphany bring clarity to the dust-filled track. At last, I can see beyond the ocean of me.

Now as I face the mirror I know that the image is not abstract but rather the reflection of my true self. The peace I have sought has always been inside of me. The serenity I continue to seek has its origin and fulfillment within the canyon of who I am authentically, not who the world expects me to be. I realize I've been running away from something all my life. Likewise, I've been running toward something. The unrealistic thoughts of complete atonement after living an imperfect life, where plenty of good company resides, is outweighed only by plunging into the sea of forgiveness and not looking back. My winged feet and bustling muscles are accompanied by a heart not so pure, but cleansed through forgiveness. The freedom that self-forgiveness offers bears the heavy cost of reflection and awareness of brokenness, but I willingly pay. I declare and decree that I forgive me.

Sawubona

We all have moments of blindness when we look and cannot see, and it's up to us to open our minds' eyes and see beyond the vision of sight. *Sawubona* is the African greeting meaning, "I see you; I took time and really see you and acknowledge you for you." If we could all take a little time to see each other--not the stereotypes, not the shells which cast judgment in the eye of the beholder--rather we really see each other. We have been conditioned to think that people should be a certain way, look a certain way, be a certain color, dress a particular way, conform to a "normal" that the world sets for us. When we see others or ourselves walking outside these imaginary boundaries, we are quick to judge and slow to accept.

The year was 1971, and my eighth-grade year carried a suitcase filled with integration, race riots, new school, sports, and a lot of "us versus them." This was the same year Marvin Gaye came out with the hit, "Mercy, Mercy Me," and while this song was about environmental racism, you can certainly apply the wording to racial injustice. For me, it was the year of the big afro, bell-bottom pants, image and reputation, soul music, and yes, girls. The kids in my all-black neighborhood were bussed to an all-white school in an all-white neighborhood. Public school in the inner city was challenging enough without adding integration, daily fights, and the struggle to belong to its complexity. While many things kept people separate amidst integration, one of the few things that brought people together was sports. Whether you played or was a fan, sports had a way of bringing people together, if only for the moment of an event. More interracial friendships came together on fields, courts, rinks, and courses than anywhere else. During a game, you would think we were all best friends, but as soon as it was over, we would separate by color and you would think we were the worst of enemies.

I was bigger and stronger than most, so no one ever picked a fight with me. Also, with the strictness of my parents, fighting in school or anywhere wasn't a risk I was willing to take. Between classes there were race fights and race riots that I would walk through untouched, not touching anyone. I was hardened by the cruelty the world had brought to my doorstep, and this violence became the new normal in daily life. My daily routine consisted of school, avoiding fights, integration with separation, sports, homework, bed, and repeat. One day after basketball practice, five of us black guys were walking home through a white neighborhood. Two white policemen stopped, got out of their car, drew their guns, and pointed them at us, forcing us on the ground. This was the first time anyone had pointed a gun at me, and to say it was horrifying is an understatement. They questioned us, asking why we were walking in that neighborhood. Then, they called the school to verify that we were who we said we were and that we had just left basketball practice.

Eighth-grade children forced on the ground by police with guns...it was a day to remember for sure. When they finally let us leave, we continued home in silence. All five of us--having experienced racial profiling first-hand--were traumatized. To think one wrong move or one wrong word and all of us could have lost our lives for doing nothing other than being black! For me fifty years would pass before I would speak of this incident. Looking back, I ponder. Was it my fear that led me to this dark road or was it the police officers' fear and lack of cultural intelligence that led them to make the road dark?

Music is the soul and storytelling of the times, and if we listen to Marvin Gaye's song, "Mercy, Mercy Me" and apply those words to race relations in the early seventies, what story is the song telling us? The words tell a story of injustice to the environment, but to me, they speak to the injustice of people. Even today, they represent a cry of black people for mercy. I encourage you to Google the lyrics to "Mercy, Mercy Me."

Chapter 3

Razor's Edge

Holes

Where I grew up, a boy was considered to have arrived once he could go to the park, or as we called it, The Wreck, by himself. The wreck is where you could watch some of the best basketball players in the city of Houston, maybe even the state. Rarely could you pass by and not see a game or two going on, day or night. This is the place where neighborhood and city stars were born. It was also a birthplace for other things like trouble, drugs, fights, and certainly it was the epicenter for trash talking.

To be able to go and watch and not be disrespected was, of itself, an honor, and if you were picked to play in a pickup game you were considered extraordinarily talented. The younger kids were not allowed to even think about playing, and the only time they did play was when the courts were empty. Most kids, if allowed to watch, were witnesses to greatness in the skills of not only basketball, but teamwork, connection, courage, strength, speed, and coordination. The court had a concrete floor and rarely were the nets in good shape if they were on the baskets at all. There were two main baskets that made up the whole court and then there were four side baskets for those not ready to play full-court. Bleachers surrounded the court, and to get a seat, you had to be somebody.

I was seldom allowed to play beyond the street where I lived, and the leash that Mama held tightly did not extend to The Wreck until she felt comfortable that I was of age and prepared for what might come. The Wreck was only three blocks from my house, but it might as well have been three-hundred miles away. The only way I could go was with my older brother as my guide and protector, but Craig was more into football and books. More than any of my other siblings, he was the thinker of the family and the wreck was neither academically challenging nor intellectually stimulating enough for his liking. All the other kids my age went to The Wreck unaccompanied, and the day finally came when, without permission, I joined my homies. In the adolescent mind of a ten-year-old, I was a man and ready to take on the world. The world of basketball was waiting for me, and I thought I had arrived. On what I thought would be the best day of my young life, finally I had friends to hang out with, and we were watching what seemed to be the NBA championship. This was the day Cyrus would start to leave his mark on The Wreck. Little did I know this would be the day The Wreck left its mark on me.

The speed of the game and the players, how high they could jump and dunk the basketball, and incredibly accurate passes were all overwhelming for me. I sat in delight watching, listening, learning, and wishing one day I could play, that one day I would be picked. Then out of nowhere, a car sped through the parking lot and abruptly stopped. An outraged driver exited the car holding a shotgun. As he quickly approached the courts, yelling, we could tell he was having a serious argument with one of the guys on the court. We would later find out that this dispute was over a girl, and that would be another lesson learned by me from The Wreck. As they argued, the one with the gun kept walking toward the other one forcing him backward. Then, even before I could hear gunfire, I saw the one guy lifted in the air and flying backward. It was as if everything was moving in slow motion and moving fast at the same time. The guy with the gun ran back to his car and sped off. We all ran to the guy who was shot and lying on the ground. He was screaming, "It's burning, it's burning!" and we could see what appeared to be thousands of little holes, and in the holes we saw the pink flesh beneath his skin and then blood began to squirt. It was like nothing I had never seen, a man shot and the horrific damage to a body that a gun can inflict.

After some time, an ambulance came and picked up the victim. Although he survived, he would endure lifelong complications that eventually would cause his death some years later. The shooter was captured by the police and went to prison for many years. They weren't the only victims. There were all of us who witnessed this event. I cannot say how it affected my homies, but it was traumatic for me. Fifty-four years later, I still cannot imagine how a person can use a gun to harm another human being. I still see the holes. I see the holes in this world as we hurt and kill each other with lack of empathy and kindness. I see the holes of inequality and exclusion, and I see the pain and consequences for the children of this world. I see the holes of bad relationships and how division and deception wreak havoc on our world. I see the holes in me and my brokenness even today as I continue to be affected by the lessons of The Wreck.

A day that I thought would be the best day of my life became one of my worst days and has stayed with me throughout my life. The Wreck was not just a playground with a basketball court. It was a living, breathing thing; it was a teacher; it was a giver and a taker; it was power; and it was humility; it was a maker and a marker; it was the mountaintop and the valley; it was a place of reckoning, a place that could wreck you or make you stronger. Those who dared to go to The Wreck either survived and became stronger or fell victim to its mystique. The Wreck broke me then it built me back up and made me better. Your wreck can be a playground, a school, a family, a gang, a group of friends, or a romantic relationship. It can be anything or anyone. We all have wrecks in our lives, and it is not the impact but the resolve that a wreck gives us that makes us worse or makes us better. The choice is ours.

I Could Hear Her Silence

In a world filled with violence and hatred, injustice and inequality, anger and atrocities, deep in a small Southern Louisiana town I could hear the silence of my grandmother, Momo. Far off the beaten path on the lonely Catahoula highway, my grandparents and two spinster aunts lived on a thirty-three-acre tract of land. The unspoiled air was filled with the sweet smell of sugar cane from the fields that surrounded them. Relatives bordered their land from both the north and south; and generations would build homes on these properties, work the fields and tend livestock. It was a remarkably simple-looking life from the outside, but inside turmoil covered the struggle of failed attempts at a fair chance for justice and opportunity. Clinging to hope and surviving on sheer will, they did whatever they needed to do to provide basic needs. Love of family was the center of existence, and belief in something greater than themselves was their resolve.

Momo was a pretty, light-skinned, Creole woman who wanted nothing, complained never, and cherished her family always. She wore the same few dresses every day, draped with an apron around her waist. Her only trips outside the farm were her twice-daily visits to Madam Quincy, an elderly woman she worked for. It was a two-mile walk each way, and she did her four miles barefoot. There were only two times I ever saw Momo in shoes, once when she went to town for my grandfather's funeral, the second time was her funeral. These were also the only times she ever left the farm. Momo's job consisted of cooking and cleaning and various other household chores. It was the 1960s and early 1970s, and back in those days, a black woman doing house chores for an elderly white woman received meager pay, at best.

Momo's native language was Creole, but she learned to speak English for the sake of communicating with her grandchildren. When her youngest grandchild became a teenager, she told all of us she would no longer speak English, and said if we wanted to talk to her, we would have to learn to speak her native tongue...which we did. I think this was her way of preserving a dying language from a dying culture, a culture she held close to her heart.

Momo carried a cane knife everywhere she walked. She used it to cut weeds, cut sugar cane, kill snakes, cut rope, and pick up things. To her, the cane knife was like the staff to Moses--an ever- present, all-useful, all-powerful tool.

Momo never stopped working from sunup to sundown every day of her life. She was a soft-spoken woman of few words, but every word she spoke counted. It was in her silence that we could hear her the loudest. In her silence, she said, "I will work for you because I love you." In her silence, she said, "I will do without shoes so you can have shoes." In her silence she would work with sores on her feet and bear the pain for the good of her family. In her silence she said, "I will wear the same clothes every day so you can have clothes." At night on her knees, in her silence she said, "I believe in something greater than myself." In her silence she said, "I will give my last penny and even die for you, so you will have what you need." In her silence she said, "Do not forget me, I am Creole, I am family, I am love." In her silence she said, "I am Momo." She showed us that it is not about the words you speak or the things you have. It is about the actions you are willing to do for another.

He Gave His All

He counted every penny, and he made every penny count as he gave all he had. All he had to give was himself. My father was a hard-working man, and with no more than a second-grade education he went beyond what most people in similar situations could ever imagine. Pulled out of school by his parents to help his family in the town of Cecilia, Louisiana, my father worked the fields and took care of the cows and other livestock, especially horses. He was conditioned to work tirelessly from sunup to sundown seven days a week three-hundred sixty-five days a year without complaint. Baked by the smoldering heat of Southern Louisiana and toughened by farmwork and odd jobs that paid black men pennies on the dollar, his chiseled body was hard but his heart was light. Giving his all was at the very fabric of who he was.

His name was Joseph Bennet Cormier. Nicknamed JB, his Creole name was Yuhbee, which, in later years, was turned into BB by his grandchildren. A man with no education looking for his place in the world, Joseph was a dreamer of big dreams. Moving to Houston in the early 1950s was no easy task. With little money and plenty of dreams he found work on the waterfront where a man of any color--with or without an education--could make a good living, and if he were frugal, he could enjoy the comforts of the middle class. Like farming, being a longshoreman (as they were called) was another job involving intense labor, heavy lifting, many safety hazards, and unprotected from the weather. But my father, who was conditioned and equipped to handle those conditions, excelled. Most men who worked there had little-to-no education and a vast majority of them were ex-cons. Neither category was excluded from working on the docks with the potential to achieve a degree of financial freedom and comfort. Along with long days, he worked some nights and weekends. JB also owned a fish market where he sold seafood on both retail and commercial levels. Weekly, he would pick up different seafood products from Houston and drive to New Orleans then to Dallas and back to Houston.

JB knew the power of education as well as the limitations of not having an education. He ensured that all his children not only graduated from high school but were financially equipped to go to college. He showed us his commitment to the power of learning as he enlisted in night school to learn to read and write. He felt it was important not only to attain these skills but to show his children the importance of it. After dinner, our family would sit and read together, and he would not be excluded from this activity. I can still see the pride on his face when it was his turn to read and could hear in his voice the sense of achievement with every word. He made sure we understood that any grades less than A were unacceptable. All of his children graduated at the tops of our classes and went on to college.

JB was known throughout the neighborhood as a tenacious worker and not one to cross as he was not fearful of anyone or anything. JB was also known for finding work for any man who was willing to work and would get them jobs on the waterfront and other places. He consistently helped blacks who moved to Houston and were looking for work. JB was also unforgiving. If you didn't work hard or if you crossed him, he would cut you off for life.

After retiring from both the waterfront and his seafood business, he continued to dream and find ways to make money, anything from using a tractor to cut and clean commercial properties to selling pallets. He never stopped working throughout the entirety of his life until age and time caught up with him and illness consumed his days. He was a man of few words, but his heart was big, and he was able to find a way for all five of his children to attend college. He bought us cars, fed, and housed us as well. This is remarkable by any standard but especially given his humble start and the limitations that life dealt him. His insistence for hard work, dreaming, and trying ended only when his life was no more.

Relaxing vacations, going to sporting events, watching TV, and things of pleasure were limited by his own choosing. The only event he ever attended or watched on TV was a Muhammad Ali fight. He adored Ali more for what the man represented outside the ring than inside the ropes, but he loved watching Ali fight, and he loved hearing Ali speak. When my father was old and bedridden, my mother bought him a VHS collection of all the Ali fights and he would watch them over and over. Then, with the onset of dementia, he watched them as if he had never seen them before and as if the fights were live. His excitement was overwhelming.

BB's last years were difficult, losing his independence, many trips to hospitals, and enduring the degradation of a weakened body. That's when he became angry at the world. Even through this difficult time in his life he continued to dream and would talk about ways of making money, about what he would do if he ever got well, about doing more and being more. He refused to see death as an option and fought until death won. In a sense, BB became Ali, and death, his opponent, was like Larry Holmes. Just like an aged Ali lost to Larry, BB lost to Death. Also, like Ali, his legacy of helping others, being fearless, coming from nothing, not allowing the system to define him, standing up for righteousness, and being a man of faith, BB was *my* Ali.

> Float like a butterfly sting like a bee,
> Don't mess with Ali nor mess with Yuhbee.
> Float like a butterfly sting like a bee.
> None greater than Ali and my BB.

The many layers of Yuhbee as a man were almost endless as were the lessons he learned and passed on to his family and everyone he met. BB was a family man and man of faith. He taught us the value of hard work, the spirit of entrepreneurship, how to believe in yourself against all odds, to learn what you don't know and do it well, fear no man, God is good, fight with your last dying breath. It was my father who inspired my life's mantra, "The will to do and the courage to be."

The Best

Every girl wanted him, every guy wanted to be him, every quarterback wanted to run like him, every basketball player wanted to score like him, every pitcher wanted to throw like him, every dancer wanted to dance like him, and every person wanted to be his best friend, but that honor was reserved for me. His name was Donald Ray Williams, but we all called him Hillbilly. I never knew why or how he got that nickname other than his wild and crazy zest for life. There was nothing that Hillbilly couldn't do, and he did everything exceptionally well. He was an athlete extraordinaire, skilled with strength, speed, and coordination. His natural talent and his will to win and be the best made it easy for him to be best in his class, even in higher age groups. In the ninth grade, he was the starting quarterback for the varsity football team, and also started on the varsity basketball team. While he was set apart from the average athletically, socially he was smooth with the girls, a smooth dancer, a smooth talker, just smooth. How he and I became best friends is beyond me, as I was not only not in his league, but I was also a clumsy, socially awkward, stiff, shy, invisible guy.

I lived a sheltered life and was an introvert because of some horrible childhood experiences. Coming from a family of introversion and reclusion, I found few true friends. When people say opposites attract, it could never be truer than of Hillbilly and me. What made us click I will never know, but click we did. It was as if we knew each other's thoughts, each other's moves, each other's pain, each other's joy. You didn't see one of us without the other, and yes, I finally had someone I could call my best friend.

Hillbilly was the kind of guy who was so good he made everyone around him better. He made guys better athletes, girls better dancers, and life better in the neighborhood. Everyone gravitated to him and he was cool with everyone, but at the end of the day Hillbilly and I were homies. Hillbilly also made me better, made me comfortable just being me, accepted me for who I was and pushed me to be better in everything I did. My search for confidence, inclusion, and self, started with Hillbilly as he showed me a path to accepting myself and gave me belief in myself. I was finally coming out of my shell and somewhat ready to allow others to see me for who I was because it didn't matter if you liked me or not, Hillbilly was by my side and because of that, my acceptance was a guarantee.

It was the summer of 1972 between our ninth and tenth grades that my life would take on another change. I had a couple of summer jobs working at a steel plant with my uncles and working on the waterfront with my dad, both of which consumed most of my days. Hillbilly was a hustler who did odd jobs, but none of them tied him to a weekday nine-to-five schedule, so he was free most days. One morning he called me and asked me to take off work that day to go fishing with him and his younger brother who, by the way, was also a rising superstar. After thinking about it for a quick second, I declined his offer and told him we could hook up after I got off work that day. When I came home that evening, my mother was waiting at the kitchen table with that look that says something is wrong. She said, "Cy, I need to tell you that Hillbilly and his little brother drowned at Lake Houston. They are dead. Sha, I'm so sorry." As I write this today, tears run down my cheeks just as they did that day. I didn't understand it then and I don't understand it now. No one knew what or how it happened. Both boys were great swimmers, and Lake Houston was calm, but both bodies were discovered floating.

In an instant my world changed, and I changed forever. I have carried this pain with me far too many years and hidden behind a smile, behind sports, behind girls, behind work. I have hidden behind anything I could pour myself into to avoid facing the reality of that grief. In the '70s black people, especially black men never sought therapy. We were tough. We had to be tough, and that's just the way it was. My fifteen-year-old mind was shattered with no place to go and no one to help repair it. Still today my mind wanders into darkness, into despair, into depression, into isolation when I think of Hillbilly's senseless death, but then I became a master of illusion. No one would know what I felt and what I was going through. I would make sure I would not have to endure that kind of pain again. No more best friends for me.

Today when I glance into the rearview mirror, I can see Hillbilly and not only what he meant to me but what he taught me. He taught me to love myself, he taught me to be confident in my abilities and how to become an overachiever, he taught me how to engage with people, he taught me to help the weak and give hope to the hopeless. Today I engage in many community and civic activities to help people. I feed and clothe the poor, I mentor young people, I write to inspire and lift people. I think what I do is a little of Hillbilly living in and through me now. It's a way to process my grief.

Inside the Walls

A beautiful young woman with the grace and elegance of a queen, rivaled only by her intellect, she was saddened by the world that led her into reclusion. Lydie Barras, or DD as we called her, lived her life in the confines of her birthplace on a farm just outside St. Martinsville, Louisiana. Never married, she lived with her parents and one of her sisters. I didn't understand why my spinster aunts, as pretty and intelligent as they were, never married or left the farm. DD had a particular beauty, one of a movie star, skin smooth as silk and a mesmerizing smile that captivated the beholder's immediate attention. She was soft spoken, but her simple, thought-provoking words sent a powerful message to the ear.

DD lived in a house with no electricity and no running water, but that didn't seem to bother her. She never complained, and her easy persona made tough living conditions bearable. Each member of her family had a role, and her role was cooking and cleaning the home every day. She made anything from biscuits, preserves, and butter to smothered chicken, gumbo, and a plethora of other Creole dishes. When we would visit in the summer, she would be the one to make sure we all were fed at least three meals a day with tons of snacks between. Every night she would come to us with a snack before nine pm when they would put us to bed. Like everything else we ate there, it was made from scratch and filled with sugar. When I think about DD, sugar comes to mind. She was our dessert queen. Cakes, ice cream, peeled figs lightly coated with sugar and refrigerated just enough to harden them without the figs being too cold to the taste.

When it was time to eat each meal, DD would serve our plates with an overflowing mound of rice, meat--usually chicken or pork from animals that they raised--and a vegetable that came from the garden. There was nothing more organic than a plate of food that DD served, and the taste was unbelievable. To set the record straight, I guess I should mention that Cajun food is Creole food from recipes people stole from the Southern region of Louisiana and marketed. Food now tastes nothing like it did then, not only because of how they cooked it but also where the food came from, how it was grown or raised. The purity of the process brought out the best of nature. When I think about the purity of the times, DD comes to mind, so sweet and pure. She was kind, strong in her faith for God, giving of herself for family, and attentive to the needs of others. Then one day, everything changed, and I was lost as to why.

During one trip to visit the farm DD was in her room and didn't come out. When we asked about her, we were told only that she was in her room. She would talk to us through the walls but wouldn't come out. We knew she watched us as we played outside her room. When we came in, she would ask us what we wanted to eat as usual but would relay that information to her sister or mother. At night, she would talk to us through the wall--the same normal conversations about school, how we were doing, and what was going on in our lives. Everything was normal except that she didn't come out of the room...not until right before we left. This went on for years and her seclusion and lack of sunshine left her skin a yellowish color. We were not allowed to hug or kiss her anymore for no apparent reason other than she would no longer allow it. Looking back, we all knew something was wrong, but we also knew not to ask questions. To this day we still don't know. Her grandmother was black, and her grandfather was white, and the white side of her family threw horrible taunts at her and the rest of the family. DD fell into despair with the overt racism that she had to endure. Maybe her reclusion was a result of racism, maybe some mental disorder like agoraphobia, or maybe she had experienced some incident of violence that no one discussed.

When DD went into this state of solitude, she began to write. She had many Big Chief tablets, the large ones with the big red lines. In these tablets each day she would write a personal letter to God. The words likened a discussion between her and God as if he were in the room with her. No one ever knew what happened to those tablets. They disappeared with her death. I would like to think she entered the gates of heaven as if she were going to school and carrying her completed homework to Jesus. DD died in her early forties and I'm not sure of what. She never went to a doctor her entire life and if she did have an illness, she took it to her grave. What could have happened and what was so painful that she couldn't even face her family, couldn't come outside, stayed in a room for years, and would talk to people only through the walls?

There were some days and nights that I would be pressed against the wall listening to her with her listening to me. My yearning to be close to her, to hold her, to comfort her was overwhelming, but respecting her wishes superseded any of my desires. Love and compassion floated through the thin walls, honor and dignity were preserved by the walls, and her faith was the foundation of the walls. What was so painful, so unspeakable, that led DD to live in a room I will never know but here's something I do know. Most of us do the same thing as my sweet DD; we talk through walls. We are afraid of something, so we hide behind walls as we pretend everything is okay. We speak behind the walls of inauthenticity, we speak behind the walls of normality, we speak behind the walls of wanting to fit in, we speak behind the walls of conformity, we speak behind the walls of fear and anger, we speak behind the walls of chaos, we speak behind any walls that hide us from our true selves and our true purpose. I wonder how much courage DD had to muster to come out of her room for a couple of minutes to say good-bye before we left. How painful must it have been for her to let us see her. She taught me to have courage in my fear; she taught me to honor her self-imposed exile; she taught me to be patient with anxiety; and she sent me love through the walls.

Chapter 4

Broken and Damaged

The Forming

Thinking about how, in my young adult life, I had my fill of pain and heartache, little did I know this was just the beginning. The many fights in my adolescence about racism, family, religion, rejection, exclusion, and grief all made me stronger mentally and physically than I thought possible. But my strength would fall short for the journey still ahead. The thing about life is that we can look into the rearview mirror at our past, we can have an optimistic glimpse of the possibilities of a brighter future, but the unknown and unforeseen of the present can change our perception of our tomorrow. Who we are and what we become are never predetermined, but certainly our birthplace is but a piece of clay ready to take shape. The path we choose slowly shapes us; how we view the world and what we put in it becomes the hand-to-clay that forms our very being. The bumps along the edges of our mold are the scars of living, and some of us have more scars than others. The chip in our sculpture is the cost of living. Big emotional events can either make us or leave cracks in the middle of our molds. It is from the painful cracks of our lives that we learn patience, resilience, courage, humility, and humanity. Yes, we are continually being formed throughout our lives, and our lives, in turn, form other lives either directly or indirectly. It is when we arrive at the intersection of who we are and who we can become that we question our very existence, our purpose, our why. At the four corners of this intersection, we may encounter doubt and despair or hope and optimism; we may surrender to fear or find courage and faith.

I had arrived at the intersection. It was a different time, a scary time, a lonely time, a time of silence, solitude, and reflection. It was a time to give thanks. Life had not been easy, but the pain I had experienced was necessary. I realized I needed to sit still and know that *I am who I am, and I have a purpose beyond my limited world view*. It was the season to stop and thank those who went before me for what they had done for me, for the lessons they taught me, both the good and what I perceived as bad. This was the time for my mind, body, and spirit to be in perfect union, to discover the authenticity of what makes me, me. As I found myself empty of the things I would like to do, empty of friendships, empty of joy, empty of direction, and empty of purpose, I began to ponder. I thought, *Is there anything in this world, in my world, that can fill the intense emptiness I feel? Is this thing called life fair for just the few? Will I continually struggle in the fight of me against the world?*

The darkness of trials and tribulations cannot be swept away in the blink of an eye, nor can the sorrow and grief that overwhelm me with time and age. But I choose to move forward wearing a glove of hope. Only then can I catch a chance at change. My thirst for life is quenched with every forward step. My hunger for self-discovery is satisfied with lessons learned from the torrid past that I survived. I know that the people thrown in my path were meant to be there. At last I know that when we empty ourselves of living superciliously and fill ourselves with kindness, generosity, thoughtfulness, and servitude, we learn that the cost for life is being paid in full. Ali said it best, "Serving others is the cost of rent we pay to live."

The struggle of thought and the pains of growing were both killing me and giving me life. Not knowing how to keep going, yet knowing I had to keep going. Not knowing justice in a cruel world, I became familiar with *just is*. It *just is* unless I change it. It *just is* unless I grow and become the best I can become. It *just is* when I give up and give in. I must become the difference to make the difference. Life *just is* unless I relentlessly pursue my hopes and dreams. It *just is* unless I become the heroes and heroines of my past and fight like hell.

This was my first visit to the intersection of who I am and who I would become. I looked to the left, then to the right, and back to the left. In that looking and learning, the forming of me came to be. I had to answer the question that everyone faces when he reaches the intersection. Which road shall I choose?

Words Matter

Her reputation preceded her as a hard, mean, unrelenting, and unfair teacher, and before I ever met her, my opinion was already formed. Mrs. Bentley was a towering, heavy-set, white woman who wore bifocals and didn't give anyone a break. From my perspective, she graded me critically and harshly. In the junior-senior high school I had attended for years, all of the teachers knew every student and the students knew of all the teachers. The path to graduation could not be traversed without going through Mrs. Bentley and her English Literature class. Known to break down the absolute best and humble the highest-ranked class members, hers was the one class that made the difference between reaching the top ten percent or remaining average. It was the class that would define and crown the valedictorian. Mrs. Bentley's class required too many books to read, too much daily homework, and certainly too much writing.

For someone like me whose siblings and I were known to be top-of-the-class contenders, the foregone conclusion that we would be successful was an added pressure I despised. Already feeling helpless socially, financially, and racially, failing to reach the top of any class was too much to bear. I was now facing the distinction of being the one child in my family not to excel in high school, and this position was hinging on the one twelfth-grade class of the infamous Mrs. Bentley. What could I do to earn favor from this wicked woman without my homies knowing I was working in school and sucking up to a teacher? Both actions were showstoppers for a boy from the hood. The reading of many books and the excessive amount of homework were not the problem. It was the idea of putting my thoughts to paper that inflamed my fear of being exposed. Would my love for writing and exposing my intimate thoughts of how I viewed the world be on display for all my classmates and homies to see? Would I be exposed for my activism; would my passion for righteousness and religion be seen as signs of weakness? Would my ardour for writing about feelings of love, depression, and exclusion ruin my reputation as a hard-core brother?

Following in the footsteps of a mother with a yearning for writing was not considered cool, so I either hid or destroyed the vast majority of anything I wrote. But I could not extinguish my passion for putting thoughts to paper. For a child with life experiences that forced me to face an ugly world too soon, the papers holding my feelings undressed my soul and lay it naked and alone before a cast of people ready to judge my brokenness. What was I to do and how would I get out of the tasks of this class? How could I manage to do just enough to pass and produce work phony of the real me?

Every writing assignment carried me a step closer to vulnerability and fear of being revealed as a closet writer. The shame that I would have to endure from my homies was too treacherous to ponder. Yet, my attempt at faking it would quickly be called out by Mrs. Bentley as she handed me grades that revealed my lack of effort while exposing my ability. She was skilled at teaching but was also an expert in the field of pulling the best out of her students. It was in her unwavering determination to force my literary potential that I first caught a glimpse of my hidden passion. Mrs. Bentley swept me to a place where my mind, my emotions, and my pain could form a collective union and face the demons of life that were rendering me an emotional cripple. I found a hiding place in the pages of my life where only I could go, where I could bring my true feelings to the world. I didn't know that filling pages with thoughts would release my pain. Articulating ideas was never the problem. My dilemma was facing those problems, understanding how I felt about them, and how to deal with uncomfortable feelings.

With my senior year almost over, I would be finished dealing with Mrs. Bentley, but the most important lesson she would teach me came not from her classwork or homework assignments. Rather, it came through a harsh and honest conversation. Keeping me after class one day, Mrs. Bentley had that open-heart, piercing conversation with me, calling out the mediocrity of my work and encouraging me to do better and be better. She told me about the talent she saw in me and revealed that she knew I had not performed to my capabilities during the one year of instruction with her. She encouraged me to release the self-locked potential of writing and said she believed writing was my gift.

I was selected to be a keynote speaker at the local elementary school, and, although I had no proof, I believe Mrs. Bentley sent in my name as a candidate for that honor. It was my first attempt at public speaking, and I was determined to be prepared. I wrote an eleven-page speech for sixth graders that was way over the mental capacity of the audience, but this speech/writing would serve as a coming-out for my literary talent, the aptitude I had suppressed for so many years. Then, I was selected as a candidate for an academic scholarship, the Worthing Scholarship, that was awarded yearly to one student in the Houston metroplex. The winner of this scholarship performed well in school, did a variety of school activities including sports, and performed community service. The grantors looked for well-rounded students on whom to bestow large financial funds. All candidates had to submit a written essay about themselves, their accomplishments, and why they felt they were worthy of winning. On the very last day of submission eligibility, Mrs. Bentley, and my homeroom teacher, Mrs. Bush, each asked me about my essay. After telling them I hadn't written one because I thought others had a much better chance of winning, they made me sit in an empty classroom and write my essay. With the pressure of these two accomplished teachers pushing me to finish, my essay was completed with the full weight of my capabilities. A few weeks later, I was named the winner of this scholarship, and, along with various basketball scholarships, I was able to go to college.

The person I feared the most and of whom I had formed an unjustified opinion, would become the person who guided me to two of my first major accomplishments. What made it even more amazing was that she was a White person who cared about a little black boy. After all the racist experiences I had encountered, how could it be that Mrs. Bentley, a person of a different race, would be the saving grace in my life. What was this phenomenon? A White person helping me during a volatile time of race relations, a White person who cared, a White person who gave of herself to this person of color. At the time, I didn't fully appreciate the magnitude of what this meant, but today I know that the person I feared, the teacher I resented, the teacher whom I thought was to be my greatest nemesis, became my greatest advocate.

We all tend to pre-judge people we don't know or understand, and our unfair judgment can cost us some of life's most significant rewards. Mrs. Bentley had a life-long impact on my life, my writing, my views on race relations, my quest for excellence, and so much more. The most important lesson I learned from Mrs. Bentley was that when we leave our judges' robes in the closet and allow room in our lives for learning and listening, we can sometimes unleash our highest potential.

Doors

My previous life experiences should have prepared me for what lay in front of me, but I had no idea how the doors I was about to pass through would both shape and shake me. Leaving the comfort zone of home and going to a land foreign to my comprehension, I felt like it would be me against the world. I was off to college where the only person I knew would be my basketball assistant coach and although I knew *of* him, I really didn't know him. Everything I had known in my life was about to change, and I wasn't sure I was equipped with the necessary skills to deal with a new world all by myself. The bad in life left me leary of people and their true intentions as I found myself most comfortable when alone. But if I were to go through the next doors of life, I was forced to go all in and go all out. The dilemma for an introvert like me would be to overcome the new, *all new* people, a new roommate, new teammates, new friends. It was almost too much for me to fathom, and just thinking about it created internal anguish.

Off I went on my eight-hundred-mile journey to what would be my new home, but it may as well have been eight million miles away, with no easy access to return or even call home. I would be on my own. Feeling comfortable being alone is totally different from living on my own, making decisions that had the potential to impact me for the rest of my life. What was I to do in a place far from home where introverts like me prefer to withdraw and escape the pressures of what stressed them the most: other people? Arriving in Las Cruces, New Mexico, a place I'd never heard of, a barren land with cactus and tumbleweeds, I knocked on the door of what would be my room. On the other side of this door was my roommate Richard. He was a tall, skinny, Black guy with eyeglasses and had a particularly high-pitched voice. He welcomed me as if we had known each other our entire lives. Richard was that confident extravert, cool in a goofy kind of way, whom all the girls wanted and all the guys wanted to be like. Everyone in the town knew him as the local athletic hero.

In so many ways, Richard resembled Hillbilly, my friend I had lost in high school. Was it fate that brought back to me what I needed more than ever? It was as if the universe cast a newfound friend that emulated much of what was familiar to me, what I had lost. Richard would become a lifelong friend. I became known around campus as Richard's roommate, a title I was not only good with but a distinction I would come to cherish.

On my first day of college orientation, I was put in the uncomfortable situation of long lines and tons of people, none whom I knew, and none who knew me. The uneasiness of this position and the thought of having to endure it with no recourse was almost unbearable. In front of me in one of the lines was a six-foot-five-inch Black guy who looked as if he could play the role of the son of Zeus, and his outward appearance was a sure give-away for a must-be athlete. Stirring up enough courage I introduced myself and Notie did the same. He was another freshman who had come to play basketball. We laughed and joked the day away, and near the end, he invited me to dinner with him and his wife. I was shocked to learn he was married at the tender age of eighteen, and equally shocked that someone who didn't know me would invite me to dinner. Neither was normal in the sheltered life I had lived, but for some reason, I accepted the invitation, knowing the level of anxiety it would produce.

I went to the address Notie had given me, knocked on the door, and a young White woman came to the door. I apologized and said I was at the wrong address and left, trying again to find the address I was given. After realizing the door I had knocked on was correct, I returned and knocked again thinking the woman who answered the door the first time must have been a friend of theirs. Upon my return, the same woman, Cindy, was there again, and I asked if she knew Notie. She shocked me with her response. "Yes, he's my husband." I was trying to hide my look of disbelief that not only was my new eighteen-year-old friend married, but that his was an interracial relationship. This was mind blowing in the mid 1970s. My circle of trust was increasing at the fastest rate ever. I now had three people in my circle, and one was White. Friendships would grow exponentially from there with basketball at the center of my world.

My years in college and living in the town of Las Cruces with its lack of diversity and small-town feel, would change my life forever. This was the first time that color was not a dividing line for relationships, playing, talking, and overall living. I'm sure racism and segregation existed there, but its sting was not in my sphere. People accepted me for me or at least for who I pretended to be. In many ways, these were some of the easiest years of my life, packed with good times, fun, and laughter. There were times early in my adoption to this new setting that I wanted to leave and return home, but my parents made sure that option was closed. Finishing college was a mandate.

During my hard times there I had friends who would lift me up, and I had coaches who would take me under their wings. Coach Drew, who recruited me to try out for the team would be a mentor and Ken Hayes, the head coach, would serve as my father away from home. Coach Drew passed away in 2012 following a car accident. In his funeral program he listed me as one of his greatest accomplishments, an honor I will carry with me until my dying day, and Coach Hayes and I are still like father and son.

The stories of college life are far too many to recount, but it was a season for me that opened many doors. The door of friendship with many I would come to know and who would come to know me. The door of trust and the people I would learn to trust and who trusted me. The door of kindness from a town filled with people who opened their homes and their hearts to me throughout the years. The door of compassion that would teach me that this door swung both ways, and it was up to me to reciprocate. The door of empathy for those less fortunate than myself and how I could be a person to lift others. There was a door of family all coming together in the pursuit of a vision. There was a door of understanding where I learned people are people, some good and some bad and character rather than color was the barometer that separated the two. The last door I would pass through was the door of pain in leaving a place that had given me so much and a place I gave so much of myself to. As unprepared I was to go through the door of leaving home and going away to college, I was equally unprepared to return home because I was no longer the same person who had left five years prior. My return would mark the beginning of some dark days, but the door of hope that college life brought me would shine and be that guiding light I would need if I were to survive the future.

Caged

Caged in the prison of normality, suffocating with the illusion of equality, and choking on the unrealized idealism of "We the people," my early years out of college would put me on a path of self-destruction. I moved back to the South in the early 1980s with unrealistic expectations that an undergrad degree and a post-collegiate basketball career would somehow fast track me to financial and social success and that marriage to my high school sweetheart would guarantee me the peace and happiness defined as the American dream. What would make me think that my bitter childhood would remain in the past and that my future would be likened to my college days, free of racism and filled with opportunities birthing a new life, a brighter life, a better life. Drinking from the cup of naïvety, I was setting myself up for disappointments where my thirst for optimism would go unquenched.

Finding a career proved difficult, and as a newlywed, I would be forced to settle for manual labor until I could find what I thought was my rightful place in corporate America. The hundreds of applications I filled out went either unanswered or came back with an unexpected rejection. I thought I had done everything right. I had never been in trouble, and I had earned a college degree that should have given me a leg up in the job market. But for a Black man living in the South, my credentials did little to enhance any semblance of a career. Then came the fatal mistake of trying to achieve my self-worth through others, people from my neighborhood and others with whom I had shared a classroom but who did not further their education. Such comparisons only fueled self-doubt as my dismay grew. Getting married straight out of college also brought many challenges. I was not mature enough, not financially secure enough, and not self-aware enough. These factors increased the difficulty of the relationship and often brought us to the tipping point of dissolvement. An unstable marriage, the hatred I had of moving back to my hometown filled with bad memories, and a lackluster job all made me fall into the quicksand of self-judgment, depression, and anger.

A reminder that racism in the South still existed quickly came to my attention while I was working at a customer site one hot summer day. While I was still in training, the first customer my White manager and I would go to daily would ask if we would like something to drink and allow us to help ourselves to cold bottled water or a soda from the fridge. My first day alone I arrived at this customer site nervous and sweating profusely. As usual, the customers asked if I were thirsty and if I would like something to drink. As usual, I answered yes to which one of them replied, "There is a watermelon patch in the back; you can get something there." This comment drew a loud cry of laughter from the crowd of White customers standing around. Caught off guard by this racist comment, I continued to work without responding, but that piercing stain would sit on my shoulders for years as a reminder of a world divided by the color of skin. No matter where I had been or what I had done in my life, I would be seen first as Black and punished for it.

My professional and personal lives were moving in a direction off-course from the possibilities I had imagined. Even though many people in my life had helped me, my focus would remain on the many who had hurt me. It was as though my mind was beaten, raped, and killed by them...and the worst offender was me. I was my judge, my jury, and my jailor. I was my rage, and I was my cage. It was not until much later in life that I realized I was good enough for me and that alone made my life good enough. I had been in a cage of my own making. What I hadn't realized was that the door of freedom was always open if only I stepped in. If I stepped into self-love, if I stepped into self-acceptance, if I stepped into self-confidence, and if I stepped into self-awareness, I would find the freedom I so desperately sought.

The Sting

When I looked in the mirror, I saw pain, failure, and indecision all casting me further away from my authentic self and closer to the inescapable trap of the mundane. The thought of living an all-too-common existence of repetitiveness--work, marriage, occasional vacations, children, and so on--did not ignite my enthusiasm. The questions of who I am and why I am left me frustrated with unfulfilled answers and disappointment. It seemed that the list of happiness did not include my name. The struggle of life, *my* struggle, was getting the better of me, and I was ill-prepared to do battle. I found love illusive, but not for lack of others loving me. Rather, I didn't know how to love myself. Therefore, how could I love anyone else? The day would come when I would find love in all the wrong places, and my ride with her would be a tightrope between life and death.

She was white as snow, didn't talk, never said no, and made my problems disappear anytime I was with her. Unfortunately, like anything that is too good to be true, she was a liar, and, as much as I loved her, she didn't love me back.

All good things and all bad things must come to an end, and as much as I wanted to leave her, I couldn't without help. I finally found the help I needed in a place where like-minded people who were trapped in relentless disease would go and discuss their problems. It was there that I met someone who would become my closest friend, a confidante who, like me, was repelled by the mundane. The immediate connection we had would last a lifetime even though we came from and lived in two completely opposite worlds. He was rich and I was poor; he was White and I'm Black; he had a lifetime of opportunities and mine were limited; he had multiple homes and I had one. My new friend--we will call him Suryc--introduced me to a whole new world, a world of luxury and unfathomable wealth, with private planes, beach houses, ranches with man-made lakes stocked with bass for his fishing enjoyment, to name just some of his toys. Introversion and internal pain were the commonality that bonded our relationship. Trust, love, and catastrophe would seal our union for eternity.

Suryc and I did everything together, unimaginable trips, the finest restaurants, and professional sporting events. We drank the finest liquors and flew on his private jet for one-day trips to different places. Money was no object for him. What were the chances I would even have a friend, much less one who liked me for me and one who would show me the world?

Once again, I let down my guard and let someone enter my life after losing my only other friend in high school, Hillbilly, to a tragic accident. These friendships were completely different than the ones with high school and college teammates and classmates. These friends were the kind where you could share your deepest, darkest and most intimate feelings and experiences, and they could share with you. These were the once- or maybe twice-in-a-lifetime relationships most people never have. Beyond the wild and crazy fun we had, our conversations consisted of the shared pain of a world we saw crashing in every corner of both of our lives. Suryc was always interested in me, my upbringing, my blackness, my struggle with racism, my lack of wealth, all things that were foreign to him. He and his wife were separated, but he always kept his kids close. His two kids, a boy and a girl ages three and five, would come to his beach house every other weekend, and I quickly became known to them as Uncle Cyrus. When I think back, I realize that when Suryc was with his kids, that's when he was happiest. It was then that he smiled and laughed unlike any other time.

One morning, Suryc called me insistent that I come to his beach house to hang out. We agreed on a time in the afternoon. I lived in Houston and Suryc's beach house was in Galveston about an hour's drive away. Every time I would go there, I stopped by my mom's house since it was along the same route. During this trip when I stopped at my mom's home, no one was there, but there was a note on the kitchen table addressed to me that read, "Cyrus, if you stop here, please stay until I return. Mama." I was unaware of what was happening, but I knew it must be serious for my mom to ask me to stay at her house, so I did. I then attempted to call

Suryc to let him know I would be late, but an unfamiliar voice answered the phone. I asked to speak to Suryc and the voice on the other end said that was not possible. When I asked her who she was, she said she was the maid. I found that very curious as I knew he didn't have a maid, and I immediately related that to her. She said she was hired to be the maid for the day and that any other information I wanted she was not at liberty to discuss. This was all very confusing to me, but during the pre-cell phone era, there was nothing I could do but wait.

Upon my mother's return, she informed me that Suryc's life was no more, that he had committed suicide. This was the second time in my life I had found a close friend and the second time in my mother's kitchen that she would tell me my friend was dead, the second time a friend called me the morning of his demise, the second time I felt guilty that I didn't save him. It was the second time my soul was pierced with the grief of losing a best friend, the second time I felt I should have been there and somehow could have prevented the tragedy. But, even with all the similarities, this time it was different. Back in the 1980s suicide was not a common occurance. I couldn't comprehend what my mother was telling me. Suicide was something you read about in books, but no one knew anyone who would end their own life.

I went to Suryc's memorial service grieving and still in shock, not knowing anyone but Suryc's wife and two children. Following the service, I was invited to the affluent home of his wife with other socialites of the Houston area, all of whom I didn't know, all White. During this gathering, one of Suryc's kids, Mike, sat on my lap, looked up at me and asked in front of what I felt was an intimidating crowd, "Uncle Cyrus, why did Daddy kill himself?" Everyone in the room looked at me. As a twenty-something-year-old, I was incapable of answering a question like that and can't even remember how I responded to this five-year-old child. But I will never forget the question. The question would follow me, push me, silence me, and finally break me. It replayed in my mind over and over again, and there was only one way I knew to silence the question and the pain, and that was to re-engage with my white-as-snow girlfriend. I had her in the morning, I had her for lunch, I had her for dinner, and in fact every waking moment. She was in me, and I was in her. Months of isolation went by, and no matter who tried to talk to me and help me, I wasn't having it.

I had lost so much weight as to be unrecognizable. I didn't care about anything or anyone, especially about myself or about living. I was losing my mind.

My wife tried helping me, but her words fell on deaf ears and there was only so much she could offer to help my brokenness. After all the pain I inflicted on her, it was amazing that she even tried to help me. My dad, a man of few words, told me to either get busy living or get busy dying because my behavior was killing my mom. My mom tried and tried, but nothing she could say helped. Talking only made things worse for me. One day, in the middle of the week, she asked me to go to church with her...the last place I wanted to go. This was a time when churches could leave their doors open to the public, so people could just come in and pray. I immediately told her no, but she was relentless. Eventually I succumbed to her request, and we went to this Catholic co-cathedral in downtown Houston. This was the largest and wealthiest Catholic church in the Houston metropolitan area, and just happened to be the same place of my dehumanization as a child where I was not allowed to go to the restroom and peed on myself in front of my classmates.

My mother and I sat on the front row of this empty church, and she simply held my hand, never speaking a word. It seemed as if we were there for hours just sitting in silence with my mother holding my hand as if I were that same ten-year-old boy who cried after he urinated on himself in a classroom on those same grounds. Why would she take me back to the scene of my humiliation from some eighteen years prior? Why would we sit in a church with no one there, and just hold hands at a point when my life was hanging in the balance?

I'm not going to say I heard a loud voice or that I saw a burning bush, or that a bright light appeared, but I will tell you this. As I sat there in silence for hours holding hands with my mother, an indescribable peace consumed my being, relaxed my mind, and lightened my heart. It was as if my stillness stilled the whole world, it stilled my mind, and it stilled my soul. In the very place where I had wanted to die many years earlier from one traumatic incident I now wanted to live after another horrific event.

My healing began that day. I've always wondered if it was the place, if it was a mother's love flowing from her hands to mine, if it was some divine intervention, or if it was simply my strong will to live that saved me. Was this all a coincidence, was it the universe, was it destiny, or was it just what it was? I may never know the answer, but I don't believe in coincidences, nor do I believe that destiny is preordained. I believe in the power of a mother's love; I believe we are all challenged throughout life in one way or another; and I believe that as many people are out to hurt you, there are just as many ready to help you. When that happens, I believe we should all pay it forward.

I've learned that life's lessons are presented for our growth, and the tougher the lesson, the greater the growth if we allow ourselves to learn from it. From my lessons I have learned we all have a purpose in this life, and we are gifted to fulfill our purpose if first we seek it, secondly, we discover it, and finally, we become it.

Acknowledgements

This book and my life made possible with the inspiration, help and love from the following:

Odette Cormier
Joseph B Cormier
Lionel Barras
Antoinette Barras
Lydie Barras
Lynn Underwood
Jeanne Johansen
Cindy Freeman
Weldon Drew
William Cunningham
Craig Cormier
Ed Lull
Sharon Dorsey
HTP Authors Tuesday Marketing Group
Harry Wiltz
Nicholas Cormier
Bridget Cormier – The love of my life that has been with me on my life's journey through the fire.

About the Author

Cyrus Cormier is a father, husband, writer, speaker, activist, mentor, and both a student and teacher in the principles of leadership. He has worked as an executive in corporate America for the past 41 years. Now retired, his focus has shifted to writing in the areas of legacy, social/racial justice, religion, spoken word, and poetry.

His first book, *Wandering Through the Fire (Volume 1)*, reveals his journey through adversity to give others hope in difficult times. It demonstrates the resilience and perseverance necessary to overcome adversity.

Cyrus completed his Bachelor of Arts degree from New Mexico State University where he was a student athlete. His experiences as a leader on the basketball court helped him craft his skills in the business world. He later went on to complete executive education at Vanderbilt University.

In his spare time, Cyrus enjoys writing, perfecting his swing on the golf course, and spending time with his wife, Bridget, and son, Nicholas. He also serves as the president of the *Twelve Plus One Heart Foundation* providing scholarships to underserved students based on need. Cyrus works in a variety of other civic and church initiatives fighting environmental injustices and providing for the less fortunate.